WORRISOME CREATURES

poems

WORRISOME CREATURES

poems

KATE SWEENEY

MADVILLE
PUBLISHING

LAKE DALLAS, TEXAS

ACKNOWLEDGMENTS

Grateful acknowledgment is made to the editors and readers of the following publications in which poems in this collection have appeared:

Anomaly Literary Journal: "At the Obstetrician's Office," "Why My Grandmother Reminds Me of Sylvia Plath"; *Best New Poets 2009* and *Rattle*: "Death of the Hired Hand, Hiawatha, Kansas"; *Better Accidents*: "Before Moving to Florida," "Brief Observations of Self, Age 25," "Halloween," "Kafka in the Everglades," "To Bartolomé García de Nodal, Captain of the *Atocha*, September 4, 1622," "Tongue," "Topeka Boys"; *Cincinnati Review miCRo Series*: "Postpartum"; *Crab Orchard Review*: "An Education in Steel, Cleveland 1969"; *Creative Pinellas' Art Coast Journal*: "Three Carrotwoods," "Mistaken," "Ode to My Unfriendly Neighbor"; *Flint Hills Review*: "The Map Room Bar"; *Foothill Journal*: "Dreaming of Exes," "Epithalamium"; *Hayden's Ferry*: "Two-Year Drought"; *New Ohio Review*: "Meg Francis"; *Poet Lore*: "Totem"; *Poetry East*: "On Hearing an Old Friend Works in the Mass General Burn Unit"; *Ragazine*: "Estuary," "The Fiesta Queen, or a Brief History of Florida"; *Spoon River Poetry Review*: "Nerve," "Swell"; *Sweet: A Literary Confection*: "Advice to a Young Son in April," "The Grief Orchard"; *Wordriver*: "To Skin a Rabbit," "To the Statue of Christopher Columbus, Tampa Theatre."

TABLE OF CONTENTS

WORRISOME CREATURES

STARTLE

There is usually a field
beyond a stretch
of shambling fence,
usually a deer, so close
we see the beauty marks
of ticks on her face.

And although we expect her,
she always comes as a surprise,
fragile as an apparition.
So we stay quiet
as the fog draws its cloak
around this scene,

and the first sun waits
to burn through
and expose us all
standing on spindle legs,
eyes wet, waiting
for the other to spook.

*

Totem

At the spiritualist church, my mother says, they preach
that everything is a sign that you see as a sign.
I remind her, again, because we're sort of drunk
and becoming reckless with this conversation,
that I didn't *see* anything. I had been in that black awake,
where you are aware there is another world,
that sunlight is just starting to write itself
on the eastward wall. Still, I tell her, it was there
in my room, on *this* side of things, and it said my name,
twice. I don't see the problem, she says. I explain
that no one I know—who's dead—would call me *Kate*.
My grandpa would say, *Kathleen*. My grandma, *Katie Jo*—
the grandma, who, when she was a child, dragged
her playmates into the chicken coop she used for a playhouse,
down through the hatch into the sour air common to fowl
raised on cheap feed. After they burned down the coop
one dry summer while playing with matches,
she said the chickens tormented her dreams.
They could speak, she'd said. Sentences, questions.
One could sing, beautifully. It was horrifying.
So there you go, my mother says, waving a hand before her,
as if slipping a tarot card from the deck.
At the spiritualist church, she repeats, they preach that
if you speak of something, aloud, you give it life and power.
I think, now, how they all know I'm listening and will congregate
every night in my bedroom: my grandmother's chickens,
my first cat who died as I squeezed a wet cloth into her mouth
when she was too old to lift her head, snakes I'd sliced
in half with the edge of the shovel, the squirrel caught
under the tires of my jeep suddenly able to assure me
that it was nobody's fault.

ODE TO MY UNFRIENDLY NEIGHBOR

—Mackenbach, Germany

In a different country he would be
just another old man with a gun,
surveying his acreage,
sighting up crows for target practice.
But the quiet equality of socialism
has disarmed and penned him
to this third-story balcony
where he hangs birdfeeders that swing
like lanterns from gravediggers' poles.
He is of the age now where, from a distance,
it is difficult to tell him from a woman,
his breasts low and flat behind the flap of overalls.
He prefers the starlings, punctual as Germans
to the seed that falls to the grass below,
how they inflate upwards
and suck back together in the sky
like a giant, black lung. Sometimes
you are the parchment, and sometimes
you are the print—the checkmarks
of sparrows on the laundry list of dusk.
And sometimes you find each other
standing on the porch in the same moment,
both staring down the cross-armed night.

On the Feast of the Assumption

The ice cream trucks capitalize,
their ballads more American ambulance
than German cradlesong.

The neighborhood boys run to it,
offering Euros from their socks
as if they were sacred wafers.

In another ancient town, the pious pour
out of tour buses, line up to kiss a box
that holds the black rib of some saint.

On the Feast of the Assumption,
I rock my son to sleep, sing
down will come baby, cradle and all.

I am so devout, I forget to close
the window and by morning must pluck out
the dandelion seeds that have shared his bed.

MOCKINGBIRD

You do not break the day
so much as begin
to chip away at it
with your icepick beak.
On its tip, a song as unique
as a racehorse's name,
the refrain as short as its jockey.
By afternoon, you stage
a telenovela with the blue jay,
whose call is the retch
of packaging tape ripped
from the roll.
The pen knives of your tails
puncture my sadness.
I envy how, unlike me,
you do not simply move
from thirst to thirst;
how the only thing at stake
in your silence
is a diamond for a baby.

AT THE OBSTETRICIAN'S OFFICE

—for my son

We discuss options for your circumcision.
The plastibell which doesn't ring
or the traditional method, blood droplets
on tiny squares of gauze.
Both pull the skin back and coax the pink nub
into the world to be called to council
in future matters of the head and heart.
Outside your nursery, a bird of paradise
begins to cartwheel out of its bract.
Soon it will stand, overdressed and alone,
at the helm of its canoe, cloudy sap
dripping from starboard. The hours dilate.
Behind the doctor's head, O'Keeffe's *Red Poppy*:
the petals season the air with iron
while the center's dark eye awaits a decision.

BIRTHDAY

A little of us is always stuck here, perhaps even
as far back as the birth canal, trapped between hips,
where the curved sheets of unfused skull shift and grind
like tectonic plates, the first of many quakes in life
which split open the darkness and shake us alive.

My son was born with a ridge across his head,
a tiny cliff above his forehead where his hair fell—
like the rest of us—into his servitude. My mother
wrung her hands over whether it would stay that way,
tried to hide with knit caps the proof
that gates are sometimes left unlatched, that all equations
do not solve for x. That the decisions of everyday life
are not always choices but instead a series of narrow escapes.

Perhaps she remembers the day she was born,
how my grandmother bit the fingernails off her tiny hands,
spit the chips of keratin onto the hospital floor to glitter
like moon snail shell, creating a constellation to wish upon
while still putting distance between the clawer
and the clawed. Proof that all we ever want is a way out.

ESTUARY

— for Alison, pregnant with twins

For the first time there is too much of you
in that tiny orbit of which God crowned
you the bald and sticky Helios,
and twenty-eight years now since He said to you,
it's time to go and you went.
If you remembered that morning,
how through the hospital window
the February sun stroked gold
into the plague of honey that followed you
into the wailing world,
perhaps you wouldn't worry so much
that they might choose to stay forever
as two fists balled in the nest of your pelvis,
or wonder at how they will escape,
boatless in the estuary,
their tiny fingers paddling gravity
with nails like chips of moon snail shell.
Even a wave breathes itself
back to its mother-sea.
Even stars tire of shucking light
and burst into multiplicity.

POSTPARTUM

The thoughts, now, are sticklike—
washed-up driftwood
on a beach I will never walk,
at least not while wearing a bikini.
The scent of the neighbor's
Confederate jasmine brings me back.

I drink wine on the patio
while she hangs off my breast,
more dreaming than suckling
at the unsunned bulb, so pale
against her face still fighting
the last creepings of jaundice.
The whites of her eyes
just a tint too yellow.
You have to drink like a frat boy,
my sister, the OB, tells me,
for it to get into your milk.
Don't worry.

Don't worry. Don't worry.
My husband confesses he loves
our son more. The toddler
who throws all his toys into the pool,
already knows how to lie,
and rips out fistfuls
of our German shepherd's hair.
Just bite him, I've hissed to the dog.

But I am guilty too, of loving her
fistfuls more, how her hands clench
with such longing yet hold nothing,
like the hooked tails of the squirrels
that chew through our porch screens
and which I've resolved to scare off
someday if the kids are finally asleep
and I ever learn to shoot a gun.

MEG FRANCIS

threw a dead groundhog on my porch
the night after I stole her boyfriend.

My mother called the cops and the officer
knocked at its gut with his boot and blood drooled

from a bullet hole. *That's some good aim,*
he said. *Tell your daughter to watch out.*

Years later, I tell this to a former student of mine
as we lay in bed, a Czech twenty-something

with a secret girlfriend in Prague.
Hanna, moje milovat—which he whispered

into his phone—was not hard to Google Translate.
I imagined how she could die. A slip down the stairs,

a misstep in front of the city bus. *Rat poison is sweet,*
the bottle under the sink whispered. *Do not ingest.*

Groundhogs are not native to the Czech Republic,
so he began to read about them, learned their nicknames,

the length of their burrows and lifespan.
He signed the tiny cards attached to my gifts, *Love,*

Your Woodcock. He probably meant *Woodchuck.*
And each time, I thought of Meg, the beautiful

redhead named after the Patron Saint of Animals
and how much she and that martyred rodent

did for my sex life: how the boy I took from her only
held me closer that summer in case she surprised us both

with her .22. Or, how I giggled when my Chesky
recited all the names for groundhogs in broken English—

marmot, monk, gopher, lawn-digger, woodchuck,
whistle pig, land-beaver, target practice, dirty rat—

and how his words were met with the same burn of jealousy
even when I opened my chest to him and he fired off again.

DREAMING OF EXES

My heart is a starfish.
I lie in bed, just short of awake,
caressed by the separate pulse
in each limb. How comfortable
I am curled into the canoe
of our marriage,
that when I dream of them
they always come as a surprise,
like turning over a shell
in which something shapeless
and prehistoric lives.
I tell you how they ask me questions
or for sex, or a pen, or their boxers back,
but do not say how they dip
their hands over the side of the boat,
testing the water
with their fingers, their oars.

Brief Observations of Self, Age 25

These imperfections do not flinch
but congregate like crows.

Take, for example, my mouth, lipless as a snake,
and the way I follow him around

gnawing at what bottom pout I have
until it throbs like an oil rig,

or my blond hair splaying into extensions
of frayed synapses.

This winter is a piranha nibbling at my lungs.
Soon it will realize my heart is chum.

NERVE

Doctor holds up a red bottle cap and I close one eye.
If this is one-hundred dollars worth of red in the right,
how much is it in the left? I close the other.
Eighty-three. *Funny,* he tells me, *that you pick*
a prime number. Indivisible from its sum.

I want to tell him how this morning
the graffiti bubbled so hot in my skull
while the limestone behind it blanched to the sun.
But instead we discuss the radiologist
waiting to section off my head,
to find that pale muscle or tumor
leaning casually against the blood flow
like a bum against a stop sign, an unintentional parasite:
the Spanish moss slung about our oak,
the shaggy, stuffy wig that breaks its fashion,
if not its will to live.

I have heard of the optic nerve snapping back
like the end of a film from its reel. I imagine my eye
lolling around in my closed-lid socket, turning
slowing, navigating in space like a lost satellite.
What messages then to Mission Control?
What yellow caution tape?
What burning sunset melting the West?

Four O'Clock Makes Me Want to Kill You

It is fitting that I think this
just as we drive past the armory
where a retired army tank
sits near the main gate.

Across the street at the nursing home,
the residents spend hours
at their windows, as the ancient do,
with nowhere else to look
except down the cold, rusting
aperture of the barrel.

Then I worry less for you
and more for the war vets, victims
of the distracted daughter
or unthinking son
who has left their father there,
the old man who wakes
from a night terror or flashback
and slowly returns to the world

by touching his eyes, his chest,
a photograph on the nightstand,
only to make his way to the window
or the mirror and glimpse
the wrecked vessel and whisper
you're not supposed to be here.

On Hearing an Old Friend Works
in the Mass General Burn Unit

In my nightmare she unwraps me,
stretches the gauze from my body
with the care of a bridesmaid straightening a veil
and exposes to the world the flushed helplessness
that only flatters a baby. There is the hot light
which, though I do not feel it, is always pain,
followed by the waking I am slow, but beholden to.

I will think all day of the familiarity of fire,
the waiter with his tiny torch to the crème brûlée
or the neighbor's cigar aflame on his dank porch.
Still I ignite at the memory of the afternoon when
I stood naked before her as she drew the match head
toward the speck of tick buried in my thigh
and it backed out stiffly, as one would against the cold.

EPITHALAMIUM

—for Hayden

Not this morning, but most mornings,
you would cut tomatoes for your breakfast,
the creases of the pillowcase still stretching
across your cheek while I watched from the counter,
sitting next to The Bowl
where I collected everything you shed
each day—keys and newspaper clippings
and earrings—and put them all
into The Bowl, for you
to add to, for you
to look at and say *I'll get to that,*
to stir through like a child picking the best
Halloween candy from the bounty,
muttering *Where the fuck is that?* while looking for the leash
for the dog about to lose it by the back door, the dog
which I still buy Christmas presents for, but not you,
although you once sent me a postcard
with a photograph on the front—a picture of a rock
spray-painted with the words
Chicken Farmer, I Still Love You—which I hung
beside my desk, the picture side against the wall
because on the back you wrote
I don't know why, but this reminds me of you
and you remind me of you
today, in your oversized pearls
which I wish I could find between the couch cushions
and put back into The Bowl as the soul collector
of all which is almost lost,
and just as the preacher begins the prayer
that blesses the rest of your life,
my husband leans into my ear and whispers *Remember*
when you two kissed? Isn't there a picture of that
somewhere? That would eat my heart out.
And sometimes, friend,
it still does.

All Creatures, Great and Small

After the funeral, I drive around looking
for a road like the one I was born on,
and even though I am in my hometown,
I cannot seem to find it. The closest thing
is a two-lane strip where two locals
chase their pet chicken down the road,
each tearing chunks from a loaf of bread.
The woman reaches out her hands when I approach,
stopping my car like a crossing guard
as the pompous flipperyjippit struts the salsa
along the median. I stop and mouth to my windshield,
Fuck your rooster, as if these lips moving behind
bug-smashed glass could make this stranger
comprehend that I am a lesser creature because I
cannot know why her stupid bird gets to live.

JOSELYN, IN TRUMP'S AMERICA

—for Brian and Judy

I let your foster child wet my hair
at the bathroom sink. She motions for me
to kneel before the stool
she uses to reach the faucet and pours
tiny handfuls of water over my head.
The sulfur in the Florida tap claws
mascara down my cheeks. She speaks softly
to herself in Spanish as if I am not even there
as she tears at knots of my sun-strained
locks with a comb and I clench my teeth.

Since she first crawled into my lap
I have tried not to speak too much
Spanish to her lest she think
I could understand the currency
of her tongue, how it may likely
only pay out in disappointing dividends
over the course of her American life
regardless of what her hands will do—
wring out dirty mops,
sign legislature into law.

Little girl, there may always be
a roll or a clip at the end
of your English, those skittering seconds
when your audience waits
while you search for the right word,
trying not to separate the waters
of your bilingual speech map
by inserting a peninsula-pause of doubt,
the hesitation which risks
pulling sand back to the sea.

Today in the news, a high school graduate
met her deported father on a border bridge
to Mexico just to hug him in her cap and gown
and I cried for them. On some bridge
within herself, does Joselyn's mother
feel her baby's hand anoint my head,
hear her voice, in a fractured ramble,
call me by her name?

BIRTHDAY POEM FOR MY MOTHER

She takes off her mascara with baby oil,
tipping the greasy mouth of the bottle against
two fingertips, then drawing them across her lid
like a witness closing the eyes of the dead.
Sometimes she follows with a tissue, but most nights,
she lets the pigment make a bouquet of black flowers
across on the pillowcase. I have her Cupid's bow mouth
pulled tight into a contemplative frown, deflated pout.
She is fifty-six today, and I can see, as she brings the glass
to her lips in the glow of the country bar, the scar from where
she was bitten on the face by a dog, can remember the weeks
of speechlessness and plastic surgery, so much worry
for such a tiny, pink crease running from corner of mouth to chin
like the hinged jaw of a puppet, swabbed gently with concealer
and blushed by the lovely warmth of wine.

Halloween

Evening and the fever of sunset
pinks the white patches on the Holsteins.
In her cabin, the hot throat of the pellet stove
swallows switchgrass and dust.

All afternoon at the hospital, she'd slip open
care packages from the patients' families
with a letter opener, snapped pumpkin-colored ribbon,
defoiled milk chocolate witches with latex gloves.
All clean as a barber's blade.

She steps into the yard with the dog,
feels the first snow in the hills just beyond reach
like a coyote pacing the pasture fence.
At the side of the road, turkey vultures

rain dance in slated moonlight
around the remains of a fawn and tug at its thigh
with surgical tenderness, their shrunken heads
bobbing like paper lanterns on a summer zephyr.

THE GRIEF ORCHARD

Just this side of awake, she watches the bats
return from the sated dawn, bobbing
over the arbors to the hole in the cabin
just above her bedroom window.

She swears she can hear them drag themselves
by their calcium hooks as they build
a breeding colony in the crawlspace
above her bed. He was supposed to seal it up
before this year's pups were born and the ladder broke
and fall-gray set like cement.

Perhaps she'll mention something next time
she sees him, that occasional Sunday
at the spiritualist church in Lily Dale,
but today they navigate the pews and aisles of avoidance
like children chasing each other through a corn maze.

She lingers after the service
and asks a medium for a reading,
but the old woman only offers her descriptions
of the living, only sees something amber,
an old broach or cat's eye marble—
                    do these mean anything to you?

Driving home through the countryside,
barns float on flames of yellow wheat, the crowns
of their weathervane roosters snag the sky.
Red fists of apples beat the earth.

She has an inkling that these are the last days
of Gomorrah and all she will be able to do,
come some midnight, is stand in her nightgown
as brimstone falls
and watch the orchard burn.

LAST VACATION WITH MY MOTHER

In some paradise, we got drunk
and for a few soggy hours finally spit it all out,
                        smearing the words
across the linoleum bathroom tiles
                                and tossing them at each other
                                over the resort balcony
like gin grenades.
We loved our hate.

        We coiled ourselves around it,
                        then let it sleep for months
while it replenished all the venom
        we'd milked away.

In India, snake charmers
        will sometimes break off the cobra's fangs,
                        or sew their mouths shut
so they cannot bite.
                        But they can
                        starve to death.

So, when she asked me to come over,
        long after we'd crawled out of that tropical silence,
        saying that she'd hit a snake with the mower

        and couldn't bring herself to collect the pieces,
                        I came dancing back.
I put the parts

in an empty garbage bag,
and it sat on the garage floor
                looking deflated
                and hungry
and we stared at it, until I said,
                They can't really be hypnotized, you know?

        Snakes don't have ears.

She nodded,

        but I don't think she was really listening.

Why My Grandmother Reminds Me of Sylvia Plath

It's more than just the head in the oven,
how she first sent my mother and my barely toddling uncle
to play in the gravel bottomed playground
across the street, where they rocked
the rusty swing chains until the landlady spotted them
on her way to the mailbox
and got the key.

It's the one handsome drunk she married
who could never stop her
from fucking every other one she could find.
Men who came for the open-toed shoes
but stayed for the bayberry candles,
superstitions, and real maple syrup—
then slunk off to continue rotting somewhere,
like damp fall tucked under the arbors.

It's how my mother swatted the back of my legs
with the wooden hairbrush
when I wouldn't stand still for pigtails, then cried
herself forgiven on the edge of the tub. *I said I'd never,
I always said I'd never...*

It's the photograph of my grandmother leaning
into my mother's crib, how one hand braces her baby's back
while the other hand curls into a hook just below her baby's chin,
maybe to gut her,
maybe to hook her and never toss her back

and how I mimic this movement
when I scratch the itch of indecision
or lust, and how the blood holds its breath
as it dives down under my wedding ring and squeezes
from palm to fingertip, brushing the knuckle bone,
tickling an intimacy I never knew I lacked.

MISTAKEN

when you sent my mother to the playground the morning you tried to kill yourself the sound of her swing chains in the distance could have been mistaken for songbirds mistaken for a rusty gate left unhinged in a storm mistaken for the memory of your grandfather's untuned violin mistaken for the lambs in the barn down the country block from where you were raised—the farm just close enough that you could hear them cry in the still afternoon yet far enough away that the sounds of their slaughter could easily have been mistaken for something else mistaken for a branch arm wrestling the wind mistaken for the sheep farmer's daughter pumping out a pulse on the homemade swing hanging from the same tree

Reverse Death

—after Matt Rasmussen

My uncle puts the cedar chest
at the foot of your bed,
sticks the packaging tape
onto the cardboard roll.

The medical examiner uses the edge
of the saw like a butter knife,
spreading cartilage which fastens
your ribs to the breastbone.

My mother calls and her hiccup
is only briefly mistaken for a sob.

Your heart reaches around
the narrow barrel of your chest
to find the blood-bullet
it used
to blow itself to bits,

tucks the red cartridge away
for a stickier,
more inevitable time.

You lean over the bayberry
candle and blow fire
back onto the wick.

The ink on your nightly diary
peels away from the page
like ash floating from a bonfire log.

FAMILY HISTORY

Why did you give me these eyes?
—*Maeve to her father, Nick Flynn, in* The Reenactments

In the autopsy of your brain—which always tried to shake you apart—I imagine doctors find the spot where it all went wrong. I think it would be a red and white blossom, a firework, a merlot stain on a white carpet, a valentine made by a child. But likely, they only pulled you apart at the chest, held up your heart as if examining an apple for bruises and pried open the dried prunes that were once your lungs because those were your disease's favorite food. But I want them to find that place in your brain that might tell me when you first started bursting with compulsions—baking cookies for the entire neighborhood or beating your daughter then sleeping for days, ashamed. If doctors could pinpoint the lobe, or even which half of my mind to underuse, leave dormant, I might have a chance to snap one rung off the ladder of our shared DNA.

WHEN I TRY TO TALK ABOUT YOU

only the sick words fit into my mouth.
They sugar as if fermented, round
into the shape of pills. When I am careless,
I drop them into the sink, usually
just after I have washed my hands of it all.
They stick to the wet basin
and start to dissolve, leaving blue dye
on the rim of the drain. I must admit,
there were times I wrapped my tongue
around that metal circle
hoping to lick up the residue that was once
your synthetic hold over me.

ESCALATION

On a turbulent plane to oblivion,
I wrote an angry letter
to your ghost in handwriting
crooked but silky.

At baggage claim, I plucked
my rolling luggage
from the belt and tried to go
up the escalator

to the line of taxis
waiting to move me on,
but caught the wheels
and tumbled down the stairs

which are not really stairs,
but only pretend to be stairs
for a few moments at a time
then repeat.

My friend rubbed lavender oil
on my bruised knees, put salve
on my bloody palms
and glued the sole

back on my shoe
and in these small gestures,
either you or I
apologized.

Before Moving to Florida

One should first be warned about the cockroaches,
their disconcerting speed and dune buggy precision
over the swell of spoons in the silverware drawer,
or how they drop like Navy deserters into dishwater.

Add to the list of oddities: driveways of recycled
oyster shells by Bivalve Mollusk Paving, abandoned
pet pythons in the Everglades swallowing alligators,
alligators crawling through doggie doors.

But this is the condition of people on the edge,
where the next step is water and pale portholes
blink up into the sun from a shallow shipwreck,
waves curtsy to the shore then pull kindly away.

THREE CARROTWOODS

Non-native, as most of us Floridians are,
I still decide you are not welcome here.
I try to send you back to where you came from,
pay an arborist to climb and slay you
like mythical dragons,
only to be told if he drills into your stumps
and pours down herbicides to stop
your trio of armored hearts,
the stone wall in the backyard will crumble.
Your brotherhood of roots arm wrestling beneath it
are the only things keeping it from rubble.

I glower at you from my pool raft,
purposely bump up against you
with the scarred mug of the lawnmower.
And you keep coming up, plucky and glossy
as freshly minted dollar bills, the currency
of the apocalypse. In the end,
it will be cockroaches, Twinkies, and you.
Just die already.

I want to believe that, at each center of your rings,
you are as worrisome creatures as I,
but I know that each time I am knocked down
that you take the better punch. So, I must admire
your resilience, how you make seeds so tasty,
you can get a free ride for miles around—
even if it is in the colon of a mockingbird—
then pop up radiant as phosphorescent algae
caught in a wave of perfect moonlight.

SHARKS

The churn of evening tide smacks of opportunity.
They can smell your sweet indifference
to the natural movements below the surface—
the tumble of seaweed licking your shins,
the exfoliating shift of ground shells over your feet—
until you heed the advice on the five o'clock news
after a swimmer gives up his soleus for chum:
unclasp the bracelet from your wrist
which can be mistaken for the silvery glint
of sardine scale. Do not swim near
the fisherman in waist-deep water, wondering
why he reels only the heads of ladyfish
into his crotch. Even the most skilled
of hunters can mistake the flutter of fingers
for the fan of a fin. You watch the water
and the woman with one arm swimming, her pale stump
a wet paper cup slipped over the tap of a kicked keg.
You worry how she will she be able to
simultaneously snag the shark's gills and poke its eye
to survive the attack. Under a sun umbrella,
you wait for her blood to wash ashore, sowing
an uneven hem on the beach's skirt of sand.

STINGRAY

If you are walking the beach,
just another old woman in culottes
picking up shells for the glass bowl
on your coffee table, do not approach
the girl fishing from the shore
as she pulls up a stingray. Do not hurry
to see her father hoot and step on its tail,
a bolt of currency muted
under his salt-worn sneaker,
or the way he flips the fish on its back
or sighs as it shits on the damp sand.
Look away as the daughter shoves
a pair of pliers down its throat;
but it has already swallowed the hook.
Avoid the fifteen-some seconds
when the ray can still smile,
its Pillsbury Doughboy mouth opening
and closing in a language inferred
but foreign to the gill-less.
Do not watch the girl search its gullet
for what she has fed it
before she cuts the line, kicking it
back into the surf. That night, prepare
to lie in bed with your palms on your belly,
counting breaths: *Which one is the last?*
Do not go to your sewing box,
hook a silk pin into a J and swallow it
so you won't continue to wonder.

THE FIESTA QUEEN, OR
A BRIEF HISTORY OF FLORIDA

In the Hispanic Heritage Parade, you wave
a spindled palm, satined to the elbow in white
like the sail of de León's caravel quivering to take land.
Your sequined gown is a spread of jeweled sunlight
hushing the sea, a mermaid song calling him
to drink and live again.

You will betray yourself, you think,
to the first explorer to loll in the orange orchard
of your youth, but soon, child, there will be others ready
to risk malaria, kill natives, hurricane proof their lives.
There'll be no stopping them after that. They'll crawl
to you like cockroaches. Someone
will have to build a train.

And when Cuba turns away flushed
and you're the closest thing to Havana—
an arm's length less than ninety miles—
they will serenade you with slender shavings
of affection to the tempo of the cigar cutter's snips
until you burst from your boat-shaped bract
like a bird of paradise.

But today, just smile to the paradegoers,
the tourists heatstroked and tangy as sangria,
their sunburned children still Park Hopper high.
They will carry your memory into retirement
then, in winter, slink back to you like panthers
over the sun-wide glade.

Kafka in the Everglades

Amerika sinks into itself. Vegetation crawls
to shore like flotsam. He considers the fish
       sour, inedible,
strange lungs swollen with chlorophyll.
The anhinga dips a ruddered tail
       into the sky,

lands to prop wet wings against the sun.
He has seen such regality on coats of arms,
       such blotting
on legal pads. The first night, he sits awake,
unbuttoned. Red eyes reflect in the scan
       of his flashlight,

like lighthouses on distant coasts.
All morning, lizards tan their scarred faces.
       They ignore his flip
through the field guide, the leather cover
       sticking to his sweaty palms.

Masquerading

—After the Burgert Brothers' Photograph "Men masquerading
as pirates on Gasparilla ship: Tampa, Fla" (February 4, 1921)

Only seasoned sailors understand the science
of how water reflected in just the right light
will marble the lower hull of a ship,
multiplying and spinning
like cells that split into cancer.

It is February, so the water could be cold
or could be warm enough that the manatees
don't have to roll themselves into the rivers
to feel safe, huddle together
to create a new animal the size of a sunken mast.

It is difficult to tell if any of these men—
lounging like union workers on break,
masquerading as pirates—
would be frightened or delighted
if the ship listed and the boom suddenly swung,
knocking them into the bay.

Perhaps they are ready, have practiced
for such an event, and just before the wooden beam
comes for them, dive in in dolphin arches
like synchronized swimmers.

Or if they would simply topple like toy soldiers,
leaving the only black man in the frame
to smirk and shrug back at them from the dock,
keeping his hands in his pockets.

THE MAP ROOM BAR (BUCKTOWN, CHICAGO)

It is best to imagine these old charts
still sleeping in the cabins of fishing boats,
tethered only to the whims of the wanderer
who taps the corner compass awake
with nicotine-tinted knuckles.
Now these ancient maps
cannot deny their claims
to land misshapen and soft.
They speak a motheaten language
like sea dogs shipwrecked into Senior Living
waiting for their grandchildren to visit,
disappointed that when they show
they are sparsely tattooed
and only want to talk about craft beer.
They do not notice they are trapped
against the wall, without a shadow,
leaving only rectangles
where they block the sunlight
so the wallpaper behind them
can still be a shade of its old self.

To Bartolomé García de Nodal, Captain of the *Atocha*, September 4, 1622

Perhaps it was an omen: the llama gallstone stolen
from his poison cup while each emerald
remained pressed into the rim,
or the steam rising from the stew cauldron
reflected in the servant's black eyes
as he tempted the fire with the butt of a linstock.

Havana's breath was still hot.
The theater of the sea prepared itself.
On shore, crabs deserted the ocean before a storm
but from the fleet's vantage, he knew little
of the natural mechanics of prediction, only that
his joints ached and schools of tarpon heaved west.

Dusk curled in. The gulls plummeted
like the barometer Torricelli had yet to invent.
For all men, death precedes the instrument of their survival.
But in the eve breeze that dark art would turn tempest
the sails only cupped softly as if clinging
to the memory of the wind's shape.

THE STATUE OF CHRISTOPHER COLUMBUS, TAMPA THEATRE

"Christopher Columbus was a cockroach and look what followed him." —Sherman Alexie

Always, the artists insist on that hair—
dusting his shoulders and scooping back up,
the tip lost in itself like the swirling core of a seashell.
So many attempts at his same sour bust float through history,
each varying the extreme to which his turnip head
is stuffed into that stifling bloom of collar, or seek to refine
the tilt of the worried, sidelong glance of a balding European
(perfected later by Galileo, Shakespeare).
Until tonight, my iconic Columbus
was the sketch from grade school textbooks: the explorer
before a herd of hunchbacked Indians,
his pantyhosed toe pointed like a ballerina's.
The ink lines so thick, so unbreathable.
Even the colorless sun in the background is furious.
How innocuous he now looks among the panel
of plaster Eberson knockoffs flanking the proscenium,
his hand atop his slender rapier,
the stiff X the baldrics form across his chest.
Perhaps it is only his placement in the darkest corner
of electric twilight that causes me to notice him at all,
glowing in that shade of tempest blue that longs to be purple,
his hollow gaze sweeping the audience, looking for land.

THE PROFESSOR

At first, he was more concerned with losing his teeth
than his memory, which was still smeared on the pavement
in front of the Amish stand that sold cheese and apple pies
by that curve in the road where his mind had wandered
and his hands had followed, drifting the motorcycle into the ditch.

After he convinced the doctor he knew the date,
that Reagan was president, and that he recognized
the face of his thirty-some year bride, he walked into a classroom
and opened a book he had taught for decades,
Robert Penn Warren perhaps, but each page was blank.

In the Dean's office, he wrote grants for weeks,
popping his dentures in and out with a tongue-thrust
and suck, until eventually all the king's horses came
galloping back while he napped at the desk—his temple
on his elbow—dreaming of consequences and gravel.

SWELL

"I fed my ego, but not my soul."
—*Yakov Smirnoff*

It started with a few lost buttons,
flesh prying apart the jaws of the zipper.
Each morning, the dimensions of the café
seemed snugger than usual.
The verbal ice bath she drew him
right before she left hasn't stopped
the inflammation, the capillary calisthenics,
stretching not only out, but up:
height and water, gray matter and sinew.

There wasn't enough room for her anyway.
He will sleep with other women,
but even the tiniest of them wake
against the footboard, twisted in the sheets
like a dolphin in a tuna net.

There might be a moment of pause,
the wonder at what else could be done
if this swelling does not stop—
what he might be able to take on or hold up
like Atlas—but the thoughts float off
as he pauses for his reflection spilling
oily and opaque across a storefront window,
how it glints of adventure, whispers
of where next to sail his body barge.

BALLAD OF THE BEAR KING, SOUTH ALABAMA

There will be too many animals
in this poem. It will start
in the Blind Mule Tavern
where the wine is so sour
even the flies leave it be
and the women use clay dirt for blush,
their unwashed hair
slick and bruise-colored
like the iridescent necks of grackles.

He will come up the good road,
(which means shell-paved)
swimming through the humidity
more like a hard-bellied mullet
than a lumbering bear.

He will tell the owner he descended from Osceola,
the warrior "Black Drink,"
and smile like he knows something secret.
He will hope that explains how his skin
floats like cocoa powder on the surface
of his steaming waterbody.
Perhaps this is true.
His momma always told him
the Seminoles welcomed maroons,
even spoke some gullah themselves.

With this wolf's lie, the owner will consent
to hear a song or two—perhaps an anecdote
about how the Bear King dreams in sequences:
rows of shotgun houses, rotten rail ties,
the ribs of hungry dogs—
and will pay him in the local currency
of tolerance.

But the room will drown in whiskey,
and he will play on until
the guitar strings leave his fingers
smelling metallic as new blood,
since after enough gut rot
there is no difference between a motel mattress
and a pile of sweetgrass in the stable.
All drunk men get hound's breath.
All linger after their loneliness like strays.
Mosquitoes greedy up to the stream
of any blue vein, just the same.

Advice for a Young Son in April

When you pull the cover from the tractor,
see the black engine like Medusa's rotten head
birthing snakes into spring.
Be still as they slice by your ankles and slip
into the hay crests like iridescent ripples of oil.
Believe those seconds to be the longest of your life,

until you clean the septic tank.
Find your oldest handkerchief to cover your mouth,
the blue one you don't mind parting with—
you'll never want to see it again.
Lift carefully the first bucket
which the weight of suction will hold firm
to the earth's heart-robbed chest.
Familiarize yourself with the act of reeling back to the surface
all you were certain you parted with forever.

When you've left for town with your father
and the first calf comes too early,
let it live for an hour in a world without men,
with only its mother
and your mother,
who will drag a card table out to the pasture
to shield it from a late season sleet,
and wait, with white hands knotted in her pockets,
for your return.

Enjoy this month, for you no longer need burn barrels
to melt the frozen ground before taking your weight to the spade
by the heel of your boot.
Claim the seat downwind from your father's cigar,
and when he goes to bed, hang your clothes
near the open window, until all that lingers at daylight
is the scent of so much left to wait for.

FOR RYAN, IN OREGON

You stack spruce to make the west wall
of a barn, when you aren't worrying
or picking apples for pocket change,
your shoulders getting bigger.
The bits of dust that fray in the last sunlight
make you sneeze, make you think
about getting a good horse,
one not yet thickened by work,
just something to bridle and toil beside.
The last time I saw you, we met in Omaha
and drank all afternoon on the porch
in a freak February heat
until our noses started to burn.
When my husband went to get the car,
you found some nearly natural way
to touch my wrist and straighten my collar
so you could brush the side of my neck.
You wrote me today that you found bear tracks
in the barn and that the neighboring farmer,
who calls you Nebraska, told you again
that you were in rifle-requirement country now, boy,
and that hippies like you might not like killing
but that bears like to eat and that tree huggers
are extra tasty this time of year
and he laughs at this every time he repeats it,
as he casually knocks the mud off his boot
using the frame of your door.

Death of the Hired Hand,
Hiawatha, Kansas

I loved his hands pulling that rattlesnake from the baler,
how the thing twitched slightly, as if shuddering in its sleep.

He fetched the shovel to grind off its head, that sick miracle
of jaw still opening and closing on the rusty spade.

I brought the body to Grandmother who husked it and shaved off
the tender white kernels of tissue, curing enough meat

to feed one man. Its dried rattle is still a warning,
urging my memory to stay in the barn so I would not be the one

to find him writhing at the gate, gasping in a bloody-backed t-shirt,
while the bull in crimson-tipped horns looked on indifferently.

Topeka Boys

skateboard along the drainage ditch
before the tailwind fills it with heads of bluestem,
and wait by the track for the steel stampede,
hoping to see it drop an escapee from Leavenworth,
in neon garb, like an orange rolling
from a speeding fruit cart, but it's always the same scene:
shadows rustling in shit-streaked cattle cars,
feathers stirring like tiny, white tornados in the wake
heading west to the "Little Apple," where soon the same boys
will slip into rattlesnake boots and Polo Classic Fit,
sit next to foreign girls who smell of cardamom,
and on the nights when artillery practice at Fort Riley
clatters the windows in their panes, play cornhole
with the plink and pause of its sedated Morse code,
dying to be swept away by the Ganges.

TONGUE

And lucky you, young hero,
for surviving age twelve, ribbony and drunk.
Your parents away at their summer home
in Ostrava, you drank all the wine

and dangled a bottle from a second-story window
like a doctor holding a newborn by the ankles,
while friends took turns shooting at it from the yard
with your father's antique derringer.

And luck for you, young scholar,
your father was the attending surgeon
the night your German teacher bit off his tongue
in a car accident, and because of less

than fifty free stitches, you never took another test.
But enough of Prague, where tonight your father stands
in his garden about to light a cigarette,
while you, young immigrant,

twine a lucky girl's hair around your knuckles
and press a Czech word against her face
like a cool cloth, your untamed English
a calibrated click in her ear.

An Education in Steel, Cleveland 1969

She wipes away the soot from stacks of paper,
the seats of chairs. She slips the gray chalk
through the pore-less paper towel, bringing it again
into the world of oxidation and bleach,
the sum of all colors, and sets it back down in the ashen tray,
marveling at how the smut finds its way in,
even with the windows closed,
and the streets a riptide of snow all else struggles through.

If the classroom next to hers was left unlocked—as this happens
when the hands and minds are too full for keys or anything else
that bullies or fucks its way into a glimmer of vacancy—
she repeats the ritual, twisting the ancient faucet until it whines and gutters
like Isaac beneath the knife of God's most infamous indecision.

This is the cobalt hour: the moment to wonder
who will arrive today missing a lunch or socks or teeth,
or whose mother left for a walk in The Flats and used a bullet
to clear her head. The hour where the peepshow curtain of the east
begins to rise and the buildings in the distance, like a line-up
of headless mannequins, drop their cheap, sequined gowns.

The students arrive and shed their jackets as if slipping out
of the memory of the cold morning's walk, the cold breakfast,
the silhouettes of their fathers heading toward the bruised knuckle of dawn,
out to where cranes arch overhead like disapproving gods
and ships angle their rusty grins into the dry docks.
How well these children know the march of resilience,
which by midmorning melts into puddles beneath their feet.
For now, the brass hooks of index fingers in the coatroom
are all that beckon them.

GAS STATION AUGURY, PORT CLINTON, OHIO

To get out of town, headed west,
the last stop for gas is across from the dive
where the floorboards are patched
with blue tarp and duct tape
and the marquee missing its front legs
slumps into the dirt and slurs, *Come on in!*
Our rats are as big as our possums.

In the gravel lot, a snake glides toward
the lake where the white hands of waves
motion her to stay away. Fancying the dart
of her own arrow-shaped skull, she wanders in front
of a pickup truck and is hacked in half,
her head flung into the ditch, her jaw still opening
and closing in postmortem thirst,
as if quoting Milton.

Inside the station, stuffed mallards
hover over the shelves of dusty cans
looking for a place to nest. The beaver hisses
at the skunk, its missing teeth
replaced with cubes of yellow Legos.

It's 45 miles to Toledo where *the crows will pick*
your bones clean, the pump attendant tells you.
But they meet you much sooner, outside of Elmore,
where they strut through the fields of abandoned hope
and stab at the seeds left bare by the harvest,
the broken stalks skewering the underbelly of the sky.

To Skin a Rabbit

i.
There is no need for the knife, just now,
for you will hope to find it has already strangled
in the wire trap having kicked, throat first,
into the patient sliver of moon-waning metal,
or perhaps raced panic to the end of its twitching heart.

ii.
If neither of these is true, find a heavy, flat stick.
The natural tendency will be to pause just before the blow,
but follow through, swift as a thief,
or you will merely stun it into death-deception
and skin it alive.

iii.
Slit the belly and swing it by the ears and feet
until the autumn leaves shudder under the scattering of entrails.

iv.
A seasoned harvester's hands should still be clean,
but if you are not certain the cavity is empty
reach inside.
The lungs and heart
tend to linger.

v.
Take a bite of the heart to ensure next year's hunting fortune.

vi.
Peel its fur back from the shoulders
as you would take a jacket from a dinner guest,
a mourning shawl from your weeping wife.

vii.
Regard your hands, how the lined palms tell
of your capacity for catharsis, for a whole other
wilder-life molded from brambles, graying denim,
and bone,
which, come to think of it, you should move to next,
breaking each hind quarter at the joints.
This will help the fragile flesh slip
from the body.
The skin is papyrus.

viii.
And you are the tear.

Natural Selection

Pinfish whisper like couples do about other couples at a party
all gliding under a silvery wave of sound.

They can relay everything they know in a glint,
for there is not much tender memory when the brain is the size of a caper.

And although we do not speak it, we delight
when Mother Nature mocks the lesser: when pinfish slip

into a sand trench ground out by the tide and traps them
for seabirds, the sun a heavy spotlight on their glittery panic.

Watch now how a child wades through the pool,
parts the fish as Moses did, fluttering their tiny, salty hearts.

TWO-YEAR DROUGHT

Lettuce Lake, Tampa, FL

The lake finally dies to its sin,
confesses that retention is not the language of sobriety.

It swallows up all envy, a belly full of jade
that once belonged to the palmettos lining its shores.

Now they must watch as it blooms,
downy as a field of green baby chicks.

Sometimes, a pale pine throws needles
over the lakebed, spreads a carpet of dead gold—

which the wind quickly motions on—while
all that holds strong springs from muddy memory.

The deer grazing in the deepest ravine
wonder if this means they can walk on water.

About the Poet

Kate Sweeney is the author of the chapbook *Better Accidents* (Yellow Jacket Press, 2009). Her work has appeared in *Best New Poets*, *Meridian*, *Tampa Review*, and *Poet Lore*, among others.

CPSIA information can be obtained
at www.ICGtesting.com
Printed in the USA
JSHW040333050422
24597JS00002B/121